Original title:
Leaves in the Living Room

Copyright © 2025 Creative Arts Management OÜ
All rights reserved.

Author: Benjamin Caldwell
ISBN HARDBACK: 978-1-80581-707-9
ISBN PAPERBACK: 978-1-80581-234-0
ISBN EBOOK: 978-1-80581-707-9

The Stillness of Foliage in Transit

In a pot, a palm does sway,
Its fronds insist they need ballet.
With soil shoes on, it tries to dance,
While sitting awkward in its trance.

The cactus jokes, 'I'm sharp, you see,
But I'm quite pointy company!'
The fern keeps whispering, 'Let's chat!'
With tangled thoughts, it stirs the mat.

A spider weaves a leafy tale,
While dust bunnies start to pale.
The peace lily starts to gossip loud,
About the sunlight's lazy crowd.

And all around, the laughter grows,
From plants who share their silly woes.
In this room, a jungle's alive,
With quirks that make the green things thrive.

Fragments of Forest Beneath the Ceiling

A rubber tree plays hide and seek,
It stretches high but feels quite meek.
In the corner, a succulent winks,
Making all the other greens rethink.

The ivy climbs on every thread,
While potted sage dreams of its bed.
A bunch of herbs form a parade,
Plotting schemes in a leafy shade.

A breath of thyme, a hint of mint,
They gather round without a hint.
Telling tales of sunny days,
In whispers that fill curious ways.

With cushions piled and books askew,
This indoor jungle still breaks through.
Where laughter dances on the floor,
And plants conspire for laughs and more.

Nature's Palette Adorning the Space

Greens and gold in every sway,
A happy chaos on display.
The ferns wear hats of fancy fluff,
While succulents just act all tough.

A shiny leaf slips off its post,
And lands right next to a plant host.
They giggle softly, it's their game,
In this room of nature's fame.

Yellow blooms attempt to flirt,
With pillows soft and skirts of dirt.
A smile grows from every sip,
Of sunshine caught along the trip.

On window sills, they throw a bash,
While shadows dance in leafy flash.
As laughter echoes 'round the room,
Nature's palette starts to bloom.

The Breath of Green Inside Four Walls

In every nook, a leafy hoot,
While insects crawl, oh what a loot!
The peace lily whispers, 'Don't be shy,'
As houseplants nod and wave goodbye.

The rubber plant claims it's royalty,
And sneezes dust with buoyancy.
While spider plants weave tales so bold,
Of sunlit days and marvels told.

A fern reclines and stretches wide,
Exclaiming, 'Nature is my guide!'
With potted pals in giggling rows,
They clash in colors—who knows who grows?

And so inside these four gray walls,
The grass may grow, and laughter calls.
Among the greens—a funny spree,
Where plants enjoy their abode, carefree.

A Sanctuary of Verdant Secrets

In corners green, they play hide and seek,
A fern wearing shades, feeling quite chic.
Cacti gossip 'bout dreams of high skies,
Moss joins in, with a twinkle of lies.

Potting soil's a dance floor, for roots so bold,
Each potted pal telling tales, rarely told.
They chuckle at dust bunnies, full of surprise,
While a spider plant wiggles, oh how it tries!

The Dance of Flora and Furniture

A coffee table's now a stage so grand,
Daisies prance with a sprightly handstand.
Chairs are the judges, nodding in glee,
As orchids do the moonwalk, wild and free.

The couch is a reef where succulents swim,
Quips of grand leaves, on a playful whim.
Pillows toss petals, a colorful flight,
While a lazy vine dreams of climbing tonight.

Fleeting Moments of Verdancy

In a pot on the shelf, a scandal unfolds,
A basil in bubble wrap, secrets it holds.
Hydrangeas play poker, all in good fun,
While a timid little sprout dreams of the sun.

Grandpa's old chair seems rather confused,
With ferns on his lap, feeling bemused.
The heart of the home giggles with flair,
As plants play charades without a care.

Domestic Sanctuary for Wandering Spirits

Vines swing and twirl like a carefree sprite,
A ghostly whisper of green in the night.
Potpourri battles with fragrant brigade,
While plants on the shelf throw a leafy parade.

Dust mocks the orchids, a sneaky old foe,
As they sashay past, putting on quite the show.
The cat thinks he's king; they humor his reign,
In this humorous kingdom, they all stake their claim.

Whispers from the Woodland

In the nook where the sunlight plays,
A fern does a jig in the warm sun's rays.
A pot of thyme joins the funky dance,
While the dusty cat takes a lazy glance.

The cactus cracks jokes with a pointy grin,
Saying, "When it rains, don't forget your tin!"
The ivy giggles, tickling the chair,
Plant puns abound, a botanical affair.

Hushed Breaths of Botanical Beauty

In the corner where the shadows creep,
A spider plant whispers, "Time for a leap!"
An ancient jade nods, wise with age,
While the rubber tree plots its next stage.

The peace lily sings with a quiet tone,
"Don't freak out, we're not left alone!"
A small succulent snickers, "No room to grow?"
"Just stretch your limbs, let the laughter flow!"

Green Ambiance in a Cozy Corner

A potted sage speaks of culinary dreams,
While celery stalks plot 'green smoothie' schemes.
"Join the parade!" chimes a cheerful sprout,
"Who knew being green was what it's all about?"

The pots gossip softly, sharing their flair,
"When the humans leave, we dance in the air!"
A leafy brigade awaits the night's chance,
To twirl on the carpet, a funky green dance.

Remnants of a Whispering Breeze

On the windowsill, a basil stands tall,
With dreams of caprese, it shares with us all.
A tiny thyme muster, full of delight,
"Each day unpotted can spark quite the fight!"

The orchids gossip, dressed in their bloom,
"Why do they keep removing our room?"
A spider plant rolls its eyes in disdain,
While the air freshener claims all the fame.

Glistening Dewdrops on Furniture

In the morning light, they gleam,
Tiny jewels from a dream,
On the sofa, slyly placed,
Nature's art, a funny face.

A tea cup full of green delight,
Potted plants laugh, oh what a sight!
When the cat jumps, sprigs take flight,
Rearranging decor, pure delight.

The rug, a field of lush surprise,
Covered in green, oh my, oh my!
Guests exclaim, 'Is this for real?'
We nod and laugh, it's quite the deal.

So sip your tea and take a seat,
Amidst the chaos, life's a treat,
Nature's laughter in our home,
As giggles weave through every dome.

The Echo of Nature's Heartbeat

When unwelcome guests arrive unasked,
We hide the ferns, that's our task;
But they peek out with leafy cheer,
Whispering secrets we all hear.

The shower's roar can't drown their glee,
As vines entwine around your knee,
"Make us tea!" they chant and cheer,
While we shrug and sip, never fear.

Potted pals join in the game,
Chasing dust bunnies, never tame,
They giggle as we trip and fall,
On the wild jungle of our hall.

Between the cushions, they will thrive,
Reminding us that we're alive,
With each heartbeat, nature plays,
Creating mischief in our days.

Wild Green Things in Domestic Life

Underneath the dining chair,
A jungle forms, quite unaware,
With creeping vines that twist and shout,
Nature's party, come check it out!

Mismatched socks turned planters bright,
They giggle during our laundry plight,
A fern's elbow nudges a shoe,
'Join the fun!' they cheer, it's true.

While we fumble with the broom,
They dance around, creating gloom,
The vacuum's roar ignites their song,
With leafy laughter, they play along.

As we sink into the couch,
They settle in without a slouch,
With wild green things in our home,
Funny tales from which we roam.

Tangled Tendrils of Home

In the corners, tendrils creep,
Binding our cozy space so deep,
They chuckle as they watch us trip,
Over their wild, sticky grip.

Orchestrating a leafy dance,
Creating chaos—what a chance!
When friends drop in, they give a wink,
'Look at us! We're on the brink!'

The chandelier wears a crown of green,
A comical sight, a playful scene,
With laughter echoing off the walls,
Tangled tendrils, nature calls.

As we lounge and swap our tales,
Our leafy friends join in the hails,
Crafting memories, cheers unfold,
In this green home, warmth never cold.

The Quiet Company of Houseplants

In the corner, a fern does pirouettes,
While cacti roll their eyes in duet.
Potatoes gossip, tucked snug in their soil,
And succulents claim they're royalty—no toil.

A spider plant gives a wink just so,
As ivy plots a sneak attack to grow.
At night, they whisper secrets of the day,
While my cat dreams of joining their ballet.

Stories Told in Shade and Sun

Beneath the lamp, a rubber tree sways,
Reciting tales of its sunny days.
The pothos smiles, heartily amused,
As the zen garden keeps the vibes gently used.

In sunbeams, stories of banter unfold,
Even the dust bunnies seem to be bold.
Macramé holders share a laugh or two,
As sunlight paints their dreams in vibrant hues.

The Silence of Periwinkle Leaves

Periwinkle whispers soft as a breeze,
As spider webs catch sparks with ease.
They giggle about the temp of the air,
While a curious gnome peeks, unaware.

Underneath the coffee table they pose,
Hatching plans that only the green one knows.
"Let's throw a party!" one leaf does exclaim,
"Just don't tell the orchids, they're so high-maintain!"

Photosynthesis in the Living Space

Photosynthesis, the plant's grand scheme,
Transforming sunlight into an eco-dream.
The fiddle leaf giant sways with glee,
While pothos hangs, flipping in jubilee.

Watch the staghorn ferns toss their fronds,
As light dances, pulling all the bonds.
Plants in conference, sipping light like tea,
Conspiring softly, just the plants and me.

Nature's Whimsy in Domesticity

A fern on the sofa, a shade of bright green,
Dancing in sunlight, a curious scene.
Houseplants are gossipers, nattering away,
Whispering secrets they gather each day.

Cacti in corners, they poke with a grin,
Saying, "Water us not, or we'll throw a fit!"
Bamboo in the kitchen, all reaching for spice,
Oh, the mischief of flora, they're far from polite!

An ivy's ambition to climb up the wall,
Claims it's a fashion, not just any sprawl.
But when guests visit, it clings and it flirts,
Draping in style, forgets all its shirts!

A pot with a flower, its petals like socks,
Hoping to mingle with fancy red clocks.
Nature's own humor spills over the rim,
In this humble abode, where the giggles grow dim!

Green Comforts Sheltered from Time

A plant made of plastic, oh what a facade,
Pretending to thrive, but it lies, oh so glad.
Next to it, a real one, green envy displayed,
Rolling its eyes at the games that they played.

The succulents smirk as they sip on their sun,
"What's that little leaf? It's stiff, no fun!"
Barrel cactus pipes up, "Join the prickly club,
We'll throw a wild party, with no need for grub!"

In a pot by the table, a chive grows so bold,
Bragging that cooking just never gets old.
"Chop me, oh mighty chef, use me today,
I'll spice up your life in a savory way!"

So here sits the greenery, bursting with laughs,
Planning a heist with the throw pillows' halves.
In this living room jungle, with stories to weave,
Life's simply greener, you wouldn't believe!

The Call of Dappled Sunlight

When sunlight spills on the rug,
A dance of shadows begins to tug.
The cat leaps high, thinks it's a bug,
While I just sip my morning mug.

The beams create a lively scene,
Where every dust mote wears a sheen.
I chuckle as my heart feels keen,
Mopping up a mess of green.

Those random spots all jiggle and sway,
As if they have plans for a wild play.
The couch reclines, like it's on holiday,
In dappled fun, we all want to stay.

Who knew a patch could spark such glee?
As sun rays tease, they set us free.
I laugh as I join this leaf jubilee,
All thanks to a dance of the sunny spree.

Sip of Green Serenity

A cup of tea, a quiet deed,
Next to a plant, my daily need.
Yet somehow, it grew with speed,
Now a jungle, oh what a creed!

My couch becomes a leafy throne,
With vines that whisper, 'You're not alone.'
Each sip of calm feels slightly overgrown,
As I ponder this green, wild zone.

The dog looks up, with big round eyes,
Wondering where the snacking prize lies.
I giggle as the cat, in disguise,
Chants secrets to ferns, oh how time flies!

With every sip, I muse and grin,
At how nature cavorts, it's a cheeky win.
This sip of peace hides a playful sin,
A riot of green, where laughter begins.

Glimmers of Earth Beneath Glass

Under the coffee table lies,
A tiny world, where chaos flies.
A gathering of crumbs, a sweet surprise,
And spiders planning their grand rise.

Each spot reflects a different tale,
An ant parade on a leafy trail.
We laugh as the cat starts to flail,
Chasing the glimmers, oh what a fail!

A potted friend peeks through the glass,
Smirking at the funny, cluttered mass.
The dog lies blissfully on the grass,
While the sunlight giggles as it does pass.

In this safe haven, life's a dance,
With critters plotting their silly chance.
We sit back, enjoy the chance,
For laughter's the best in this leafy romance.

Nature's Palette Upon the Couch

The couch is like a garden bright,
With cushions that sparkle in soft light.
Each hue a story, a playful sight,
Invite a laugh, let worries take flight.

From mustard yellow to mossy green,
A painter's dream, oh how serene!
But the dog rolls in them, oh so keen,
Messy masterpieces, a true routine.

In the sunlight, colors mingle free,
While I ponder toppings for my tea.
The cat claims the couch with regal glee,
As if it's the canvas for all to see.

Amidst this chaotic, vibrant scene,
Life spills over in shades unforeseen.
We're caught in laughter, as we convene,
Creating joy with a dash of green!

Celestial Growth in Earthy Enclosure

Potted wonders stretch with glee,
Reaching for a simple spree.
They twist and turn for sun's embrace,
In this cozy, greenish place.

A cactus wears a tiny grin,
While ferns play hide and seek within.
The shelf is packed, a leafy crowd,
Each plant thinks it's quite so proud.

Laughter echoes with the breeze,
As vines hang down like playful tease.
They wiggle when you walk on by,
Competing for a glance, oh my!

With soil snacks and sunlit beams,
They're not just plants, they're living dreams.
In this jungle made of cheer,
Who needs a garden when it's here?

Graceful Vines Reaching for Light

Vines are swaying, stretching high,
Dancing odd beneath the sky.
They twist like dancers, feeling bright,
Reaching out with all their might.

One creeper caught a ribbon's slide,
Pretending it's a graceful ride.
It tangles up; a clumsy show,
A jester in a leafy glow.

With every leaf, a giggle blooms,
In this home of planty rooms.
They high-five bugs, they wink at dust,
Nature's charm wrapped up in rust.

Among the pots, a fantasy,
Of twisted paths and bold decree.
In this merry green parade,
Hilarity in nature made.

Memories of Woods Imprisoned

Once were trees, now indoors creep,
With stories rich and secrets deep.
A log sat down, began to share,
Tales of winds and sunlit air.

"Remember when?!" a leaf did sigh,
A porch swing and the buzzing flies.
They swap wild tales of open skies,
While sunlight plays, and laughter flies.

"Oh, those days were filled with fun,
When branches danced and bark could run!"
But now, they snooze in this warm glow,
Inventing dreams of where to go.

Yet through the window, whispers say,
"Adventure waits outside today!"
So every bud begins to plot,
A little escape from this warm spot.

Photosynthetic Dreams Within Us

In our hearts, the green things grow,
With dreams of sun and winds that blow.
Photosynthesis fuels the cheer,
As plant pals giggle, drawing near.

They whisper softly, share their schemes,
Basking in the vibrant beams.
"Let's paint the walls a grassy hue,
And see what real plant magic can do!"

Through windows wide, the bright beams stream,
Filling spaces, weaving dreams.
They sway and twirl, they jump for joy,
A lush escape for every boy.

In this funny, leafy parade,
Life inside is art displayed.
And as we laugh with leafy friends,
The fun of nature never ends.

A Leafy Pause in Everyday Life

A green friend rests on the floor,
It looks like it wants to explore.
With tiny curls and shades of jade,
In my cereal, it's out on parade.

It sneezes when the cat walks by,
As if it's saying, 'Oh my, oh my!'
A tiny dancer, swaying so tight,
In the chaos, it brings delight.

I feed it water like a pet,
Who knew a plant could be this wet?
With every sip, it seems to grin,
Life's routines get a leafy spin.

Sheltered Vegetation Embracing Warmth

In the corner, a wandering sprout,
Pretends it's tough, but we all know doubt.
It stretches out, seeking the sun,
Whispering secrets, just for fun.

My friends all laugh, they shake their heads,
As I talk to it while they eat bread.
Unfazed by the jokes, it stands so proud,
In the silence, it forms a crowd.

Under blankets and a lampshade glow,
Imagining travels where they might go.
Though it's still, you can hear it scheme,
Living the life, a plant's wild dream.

The Quiet Companion of Verdant Growth

A quirky bud sits by my side,
In the glare of my laptop pride.
It's heard my rants, my tales of woe,
Yet stays quiet, just watching the show.

A soft breeze nudges its pointy tips,
Like it's offering me little quips.
"Get a grip," it seems to say,
With every sway, it leads the way.

Sometimes I swear it rolls its eyes,
At my snacks and my endless "whys."
But it remains my serene mate,
In this dance of inner debate.

Verdure Against the Urban Canvas

Tiny leaves fight the city's roar,
In a room filled with sounds galore.
They twist and turn, in bright green hues,
Mimicking laughter, evading the blues.

They perch on shelves, a daring crew,
Dodging dust bunnies, who knew?
With every branch, they break the mold,
In this wild life, they're brave and bold.

As I trip over shoes left behind,
They giggle softly, not one bit blind.
A riot of color on a dull gray day,
Turning my fumbles into a play.

Ferns and Whispers of Soft Light

The ferns in the corner sway,
Dancing to a tune all day.
They whisper jokes, so sly and bright,
Making the sunbeam giggle with delight.

A spider drops from his web with grace,
Hoping to join the leafy embrace.
"I'm here for the punch, not the show!"
The plants just chuckle, "Oh, don't be slow!"

The light tickles the edges of green,
Creating shadows, a vibrant scene.
Every pot holds a secret or two,
A gossiping plant, who knew they grew?

In this playful patch of indoor cheer,
The drapes flutter, as if to peer.
With every breeze, a rebel sway,
Life's a comedy in this leafy ballet.

Captive Blossoms in Dusty Corners

In corners where dust bunnies play,
Captive blossoms dream the day away.
"Why not bloom here?" one petal sighed,
Finding joy where shadows abide.

A cactus complains, pricks turned to frown,
"What's with this dust? It's weighing me down!"
A nearby lily laughs with glee,
"Just let it be! Embrace the debris!"

Sunlight peeks, a shy little game,
Each flower competes for the golden flame.
Chasing dust motes like it's a race,
You'd think this wasn't their cozy place!

Each pot holds a tale, oh, so absurd,
Of flowered dreams and a chirping bird.
A garden within, a sitcom of birth,
Dusty corners hide a world of mirth.

Potted Poets of Petal and Stem

In pots of clay, the poets dwell,
Sharing rhymes with stories to tell.
A daffodil scribbles with a grin,
'Every day's a new chance to win!'

The rosemary's sharp, quick with a jest,
"Why are tulips always the best dressed?"
In verses sweet, they trade their quips,
While basil nods, flipping through scripts.

Hilarity blooms, 'neath sunlight's gaze,
As jade plants ponder in hazy haze.
"Let's pen a tale of the great indoor,
Where potting soil dreams of legends galore!"

With branches crossed, they laugh at the sun,
Wishing they too could run and have fun.
In this cabaret of leaf and rhyme,
Every moment's a giggle, a jolly old time.

Sanctuary of Soil Beneath the Glass

Beneath the glass, in their cozy den,
The soil whispers secrets again and again.
"Did you hear that?" a petunia did say,
"The cat's on the prowl, get out of the way!"

Herb pots gossip about the warm brew,
"Who knew the basil was trying to woo?"
Chrysanthemums chuckle, their petals ablaze,
"Let's make this a party, a floral craze!"

A glasshouse sanctuary, snug and tight,
Where every plant dreams of taking flight.
With roots wrapped in stories both silly and grand,
They sprout such laughter, it's simply unplanned.

Laughter and joy in each little speck,
As they chat about sprouting a brand-new trek.
In this tiny world beneath shiny glass,
The fun keeps blooming; oh, let it amass!

Echoes of the Garden Within

Tiny green whispers dance,
Hiding from the cat's prance.
Plants gossip, share a jest,
Making my couch their nest.

Sunlight beams like a joke,
Laughter from the potted folk.
Marigold winks, saying hi,
While the basil starts to sigh.

Cactus cracks a quippy line,
In this lush, leafy design.
Ferns giggle with glee and flair,
While the rubber tree has hair.

A jungle jangle fills the air,
Stool's got moss - it's quite the scare!
In this botanical delight,
Every day feels vibrant and bright.

Vita Brevis: A Plant's Perspective

A fern grumbles, 'I've got style,'
While a spider plant just smiles.
Succulents cozy in a row,
Chuckle softly, 'Look at our show!'

The begonia claims it's chic,
As it wobbles on its peak.
With jokes about their pot-life,
Succulents tease—'No house strife!'

A rubber plant rolls its eyes,
Says to others, 'I'm a prize!'
'We're the sassiest lot, you see,'
'Even if we sometimes flee.'

So many colors, none too shy,
Each day here is reason to try.
In our fun garden spree, we thrive,
Living room humor, oh-so-alive!

Kaleidoscope of Colors on the Mantle

A pot of gold on the shelf,
Mocking the dust with sweet stealth.
Hydrangeas pop and sassy, too,
Playfully argue what shade is true.

Orchids grimace at the sun,
'Is it playtime? Just for fun?'
Bubbles of laughter fill the air,
While the ivy hangs without a care.

Succulent soldiers parade in lines,
Against dust bunnies, they take their sides.
Chrysanthemums join in the fray,
'Who knew home could feel this way?'

A banquet of hues, a silly sight,
Each bloom competes to catch the light.
Nature's jesters, vibrant yet calm,
Our quirky oasis, a soothing balm.

Rooms Adorned with Nature's Brush

Here's a palm, tall and sly,
Sways and whispers a gentle lie.
The snake plant snickers, 'I'm so grand!'
Rolling leaves, a leaf-shaking band.

Cacti poke fun, can't take a rest,
'We're the ones who've passed the test.'
In their prickly armor, what a sight,
Waging warfare in dim moonlight.

The aloe vera regales with tales,
Of brave adventures and gusty gales.
Pothos giggles down from above,
While the peace lily sings of love.

Nature's palette, quite the scene,
With each pot, a life routine.
In this room of playful affray,
Life's a joke, in leafy display!

Stillness Caught in a Leaf's Embrace

A tumbleweed rolls by the chair,
Dust bunnies dance without a care,
With snacks strewn around like confetti,
I ponder life's little confetti.

A plant decided to take a stand,
It's now the roommate, unplanned,
With vines that creep and spread with glee,
I think it wants to sip my tea.

The cat eyes it with stealthy grace,
As if it's the prone leaf's base,
But nap wins out, it tires fast,
My leafy foe outlasts the cast.

So here I sit, with nature's jest,
A leafy friend, I must confess,
In stillness, we plot mischief once more,
As life stirs softly through the door.

Echoes of a Sylvan Retreat

Beneath the shelf, a sprout does gleam,
A woodland scene, or so it seems,
It whispers tales of far-off trees,
And cheeky squirrels who aim to please.

The coffee table's playground fun,
A habitat for leaves on the run,
Each petal nervously takes a peek,
While I just sit and sip my tea.

A quirk in shape, a twist in green,
Who knew art could be this keen?
With bold ambitions, it steals the show,
As I laugh at the high drama low.

To think of tales it must have seen,
Trapped in a world that's quite routine,
Yet laughter rings, a leafy cheer,
Inviting joy to linger near.

Nature's Tenuous Threads

A spider spins tales above my head,
As I sip tea and forge ahead,
Bright colors clash, green threads involved,
In this puzzle, I'm quite evolved.

A stray finger nudges a tiny bud,
It wobble-walks like a drunken flood,
Oh, nature's chaos within these walls,
Who knew the thrill of impromptu spalls?

Raucous laughter echoes through the air,
With petals flapping in widespread flair,
A living room, yet wild and free,
A green mischief cast just for me.

As daylight wanes, shadows grow long,
The plant hums quietly a funny song,
In this lush embrace, I find my muse,
With playful wonders, I cannot lose.

Essence of Green within Four Walls

Within these bounds, a jungle thrives,
A leafy realm where laughter strives,
Each branch a wand, each stem a show,
I cohabitate with leafy woe.

The rug's a meadow, a place to muse,
As sunbeams play her trade amuse,
While mocking thyme begins to croon,
It's just a grapevine, singing tunes.

In this oasis of fabric and cheer,
Who needs the wild when my home's right here?
With the cat plotting from under the couch,
As green conspirators move to vouch.

And each day dawns with hearty laughs,
As rooted friends share their green paths,
Life unfurls in playful zest,
A little chaotic, but I'm quite blessed.

Whispers of Autumn's Touch

A rustle here, a crinkle there,
The plants plot jokes without a care.
They giggle softly, a leafy spree,
While dust bunnies dance with glee.

Cacti wear hats, they're feeling bold,
Potted tales of mischief unfold.
One fern claims it's the king of the space,
While the spider plant just tries to keep pace.

Mismatched socks on the floor, oh dear,
The plant friends chuckle, it's quite clear.
They whisper secrets of nature's flair,
While I wonder why I just don't care.

In this leafy comedy, all feels bright,
A harvest of humor, pure delight.
As the sun sets low, it's time to store,
These green allies leave me wanting more.

Ephemeral Greenery

The ivy's creeping, like it's on patrol,
Giving those cracks some leafy soul.
It peeks around like a cheeky spy,
While I trip over potting mix, oh my!

A cactus dropped by with a prickly grin,
Stirring up laughter, let the games begin.
"Why did the fern cross the floor?" it said,
"To leaf the mess, that's why I fled!"

Succulents giggle at my terrible aim,
Throwing clumps of dirt, what a shame!
They blossom with joy, oh what a scene,
As I clean up their little green scheme.

In this wild jungle, every leaf's a friend,
With pranks and puns that never end.
So here's to the green, the jolly crew,
Bringing chuckles to everything we do.

The Nature's Embrace Within

The foliage whispers with a wink and a nod,
Telling tales of a bathroom remodel gone odd.
"Beware of the soap!" giggled the fern,
"I slip on shampoo when it's my turn!"

A rubber plant's hosting a botanical ball,
Potted pals gather, they're having a ball.
With a twist of a leaf and a shake of a stem,
They're all in high spirits, but I'm just a gem.

The bonsai tried to stand up tall,
But all those shenanigans made it fall.
"Gravity's mean!" it cried with a laugh,
While I struggle to find another vase half.

In this room full of plants, such delight,
The jests and the chuckles, they're out of sight.
I join in the fun, with a smile so wide,
Cheers to the green and their whimsical pride!

Solace in the Foliage

A spider plant swung with delicate grace,
"Join the dance!" it said, while setting the pace.
With mischief afoot, they show their flair,
Creating a ruckus, all without care.

The ferns all gather for a game of charades,
Acting out tales, with no time for shades.
A floppy leaf raises a gentle cheer,
As I laugh at their shenanigans near.

Curly vines tease, "Look, I can fly!"
As I trip on the rug and let out a cry.
"Not so easy, eh?" they all seem to say,
"Join our fun or get swept away!"

In this cozy chaos, what a delight,
Nature's embrace makes everything right.
With giggles and grins, the plants did thrive,
Radiant joy keeps this home alive.

The Solace of Chlorophyll Under Roof

In the corner, a plant stands tall,
Waving its arms, it calls to all.
Dust settles gently on its bright hue,
Wonder if it wishes for a view.

A spider visits, thinks it's a tree,
But leaves have no branches, oh silly bee!
The light shifts, shadows dance in spree,
Is that a jungle or just my cup of tea?

Watering can is ready to spill,
While ferns plot, scheming for thrill.
A chatty pot keeps gossip alive,
While ivy climbs to join the jive.

Sometimes I wonder how they think,
Just sitting there, silently wink.
The chlorophyll crew, what a sight,
Bringing the fun, day and night!

Homecoming of the Wild and Green

A welcome mat of petals is laid,
As I walk in, the décor is played.
Potted friends, in colors so bright,
Seem to giggle, what a delight!

The rubber plant is on the couch,
With a sneaky smile, like it's a slouch.
The cactus rolls its prickly eyes,
As I tell jokes, it sighs and sighs.

Succulents nod, at the absurd,
Who knew they had quite a word?
Trailing vines come down like snakes,
Saying "We're here for all the breaks!"

Oh home of green, you crack me up,
With every bloom, my soul you fill up.
A kingdom of oddities and cheer,
I can't help but laugh, year after year!

A Canopy of Dreams Inside

An indoor canopy, what a surprise,
Hiding secrets, right before my eyes.
Cushiony leaves whisper in glee,
What will they dream? Let's wait and see!

Messy adventures of dirt and grime,
A tiny invasion, isn't it prime?
Poking fun at my feline friend,
Who thinks the plants are latest trends.

In the sunlight, they shimmy and sway,
Pretending it's all just a ballet.
Fern twirls while the rubber tree claps,
Did I walk into a show of mishaps?

Each time I water, a concert begins,
With potting soil-beats and root-spring wins.
With laughter and joy in every sprout,
This indoor jungle is what life's about!

Botanicals Breathing in Still Air

Quietly breathing, in their green zone,
The plants hold court, more than known.
Each spiked leaf a royal decree,
While I'm just a guest, sipping my tea.

A gentle breeze, oh wait, it's me,
Puffing my cheeks, puffing with glee.
The spider plant huffs, "That's quite enough!"
I laugh so hard, it gets quite tough!

On the shelf, a thistle has claims,
"I'm the best at playing made-up games!"
As I join in, they roll their eyes,
But secretly love my silly tries.

Who knew a room could be so spry?
With chatter and warmth, time passes by.
In this quirky haven, I reside,
With green companions, joy our guide!

Nurtured Green: A Hearthside Tale

In a pot by the fire, it sits so round,
It dreams of the forest, but can't leave the ground.
A spider took flight, right over the chair,
While the plant just stood still, without a care.

The cat plays a game, it's her favorite sport,
With her paws on the leaves, they become a report.
She pounces and prances, it looks like a dance,
The plant plays along, giving fate a chance.

A sunbeam comes shining, the plant leans in tight,
Thinking it's a signal for plants' party night.
Yet day after day, it just sits and glows,
While the cat rolls her eyes, then lazily dozes.

So together they sit, in a curious pair,
One dreaming of forests, the other of air.
The hearth keeps them warm, in a cozy embrace,
Just a pot and a cat, in their funny little space.

Growth and Glow in Urban Retreat

In a corner so bright, there's a green little chap,
With stems that keep growing, and leaves in a flap.
Its dreams of the city, a skyscraper view,
But the window's too foggy for a clear breakthrough.

A squirrel through the pane, does a silly little jig,
The plant looks amazed at this tiny, furry gig.
It wants to go out, to dance on the street,
But stuck in a pot, it finds no two-step beat.

The dust motes are twirling in rays warm and bright,
The plant sways a bit, like it's caught in the light.
If only it had arms to wave and to cheer,
It would host a rave, let all the neighbors near!

What a disco of greenery, a snazzy display,
With pot-tapping roots putting on quite the sway.
In dreams of the evening, over juice and cake,
It plans a grand gig, oh, for goodness' sake!

The Dance of Life in the Humble Room

In the middle of chaos, it finds its own beat,
A green little buddy, not missing a feat.
With socks on the table and crumbs on the floor,
It stands there quite proudly, wanting some more.

The dog gives a bark, as he spots the fun show,
His tail starts a wag, in a rapid, wild flow.
He prances around, kicking toys to the side,
While the plant just observes, with dignity and pride.

In a sunny corner, a little rebel grows,
Beneath the old lamp, it boldly bestows.
Ferns wave to the dust bunnies, a dance in the light,
While the cat rolls her eyes, "You'll never take flight!"

The vacuum comes roaring, to spoil their grand ball,
But the plant just chuckles, "Come give it your all!"
Let the chaos unfold, in this room that we share,
With laughter and green, there's fun everywhere!

Nature's Elegance Within Reach

A thriving green wonder, just shy of the wall,
It winks at the toaster, a neighbor so small.
"Let's have a party!" it whispers so loud,
While the toaster just puffs, all covered in cloud.

The fridge joins in too, with a rattling dance,
Keeps lighting its belly, like giving a chance.
The plates and the cups, they sway in delight,
A kitchen soirée, under gleaming moonlight.

The blender hums softly, with a rhythmic spin,
While the plant keeps on dreaming, of great leaves to win.

If only the rug could join in the fun,
They'd have quite the party until the day's done!

Every little wrinkle, every quirky design,
Makes this humble room a true space divine.
With laughter and joy in earth's little nook,
Nature's elegance stirs, so take a good look!

A Symphony of Stems and Sprouts

Green spots on my table,
Where plants like to jiggle.
They dance when I trip,
In a leaf-laden slip.

Cacti wear tiny hats,
As they chat with the mats.
Fern fronds wave hello,
In a wild, leafy show.

Succulents sip their tea,
Gossiping next to me.
A garden's jiving spree,
In this cozy spree.

Rooted in laughter's grace,
What a quirky place!
With nature's wily charms,
I'm held in their arms.

Textures of Tranquility by the Fire

Near the flames we gather,
With petals as our lather.
The pot on the mantle,
Is a greenery scandal!

Moss creeps on the couch,
The plants begin to slouch.
A bamboo starts to sway,
As I sip on my whey.

Pillows bloom in the light,
Colors dancing so bright.
We joke about the weeds,
As the fireplace feeds.

Rustling quirks abound,
In this cuddly ground.
Green layers and laughs mix,
In domestic fix.

Sunkissed Tints in Domestic Bliss

Sunlight spills through the glass,
On each sprout, they amass.
The ferns seem to wink,
As I ponder and think.

Chlorophyll's a riot,
As it starts a quiet.
Green gossip on the floor,
Who could ask for more?

Blossoms on the shelf,
Laughing at themselves.
A pet rock gets envious,
In this space so generous.

Exotic plants conspire,
While my curtains retire.
With humor in each nook,
Nature's funny look!

Essence of Eden Within the Walls

In a jungle of my making,
The pots keep on shaking.
Vines twist and twine,
Even though they confine.

The ivy plays peek-a-boo,
As my cat makes her debut.
Basil whispers a charm,
While oregano's warm.

The sun's rays tickle green,
A funny little scene.
Can't tell a weed from gold,
In the antics retold.

With glee, the colors clash,
In a hilarious flash.
At home, the fun never stalls,
In this Eden's small walls.

Green Guardians of the Quiet Realm

In a pot high up on the shelf,
A cheeky plant thinks it's itself.
It sways and wiggles, what a sight,
A leafy dance, oh what a fright!

Dust bunnies watch with jealous eyes,
Chasing the green with silent sighs.
They plot and plan, but can't compete,
Against the sprout that's oh so neat!

A tiny sprig has wisdom bold,
It shares its secret, yet untold.
"Eat your greens, but do not eat me,"
Cackles the herb, quite cheerfully!

In this realm where plants reside,
They laugh and joke, they do not hide.
The guardians of this cozy space,
All with a laugh, a leaf, a grace!

A Tapestry Woven with Nature's Threads

Threadbare curtains, let in the light,
The fern gossiping, quite in delight.
"Have you seen the dust that swirls?"
The cactus chimes, as the curtain twirls!

A spider spins its clever web,
While geraniums moan, each little ebb.
"Who needs a gardener, we've got flair!"
Cackles the ivy, hanging in air!

Beneath the shelf, the chaos grows,
A tiny seedling, how it glows!
Whispers of soil travel wide,
In this tapestry, there's nothing to hide!

From every corner, laughter springs,
As nature's choir hilariously sings.
In this cozy, jumbled space,
We're all stitched in, what a funny place!

The Closure of Petals in Public Space

A flower pouts, it's nearly noon,
Shy of the light, it hums a tune.
When company comes, it hides so neat,
Behind the pots and the old brown seat!

"Be bold!" cried out the frisky vine,
"You're part of this mess; it's quite divine!"
But petals quiver, stay on the floor,
They'd rather sink than show some lore!

The cactus chuckles, "Don't be shy!
Bloom where you are, just give it a try!"
As the guests arrive with cookies to share,
The shy ones peep, a little aware!

Yet when the room fills with chatter and cheer,
The bunch starts laughing, they have no fear.
"Here's to the blooms that stay tucked away,
Open your petals; it's the funny way!"

The Resilience of Flora in the Hearth

In the cozy hearth, green lives abound,
Potted pals cheer, a joyful sound.
"We're never dull, we're always spry!"
Exclaims the plant with a cheeky eye!

Jokes and banter among the leaves,
"We're better than curtain thieves!"
Each with a laugh, in that warm warm glow,
They twist and twirl, putting on a show!

When a sock slips by, they gasp in shock,
"It's a giant beast, oh what a knock!"
But when it's just dust, they laugh and chime,
"Looks like we've got ourselves a rhyme!"

In this little hearth, resilience thrives,
Green guardians giggle, and joy resides.
Together they flourish, a jolly old sort,
In the warmth of the home, a very sweet court!

A Tapestry of Seasons

A pile of greens on the floor,
I blame the cat, he wanted more.
They're swirling like a magic spell,
Tangled tales, oh can't you tell?

The windowsill's a leaf parade,
With stories told of sun and shade.
Whispers of autumn, a gentle tease,
Mismatched socks, and a dance with ease.

Orange bits on the table's edge,
A laugh escapes, it's time to pledge:
To never let nature inside too deep,
Or else we'll find plants in our sleep!

In every nook, a green surprise,
As if the room has grown some eyes.
They giggle softly, play their tricks,
While I just search for cleaner picks.

Potted Remnants of Wanderlust

Trekking through soil in a terracotta home,
Lost in the ferns, I dare not roam.
Dirt on my shoe, a tale to unfold,
Adventure awaits, but the plant's too bold.

A cactus grins with a sharp little wink,
Saying, 'Ease up buddy, it's time to think!'
Moss awkwardly nudges, 'You're stuck in a groove,
Can't you see, I'm the one to improve?'

A fern offers gossip, a scandal so bright,
'That succulent's hiding, it's quite the sight!'
Houseplants have secrets, oh such a plot,
Tales of wild journeys, and they've seen a lot.

Still, who knew living could bring such glee?
With potted tales of where we would be.
Dancing with greens and a sprinkle of dirt,
Cheering for journeys where laughter won't hurt.

Shadows of Trees at Dusk

As sunlight fades, shadows creep,
A leafy ghost begins to leap.
I trip over roots like a clumsy fool,
While the branches giggle, 'Oh, what a tool!'

Green monsters lurk in the corner's gloom,
Surveying the room with their leafy plume.
They snicker and whisper, what a fine show,
As I untangle my shoes in woe.

A banana peel offers some sage advice,
'Watch where you step, we roll like dice!'
The sofa joins in, with a groan and a sigh,
'Can we please keep it down? The cushions want to cry!'

So, here we stand, plants in quirk,
Teaching me humor with every jerk.
For in this chaos, we find delight,
Entwined in giggles, we dance through the night.

Homegrown Echoes of the Wild

In the corner sprouts a leafy man,
Waving hello like a boisterous fan.
He teases the dog with a rustling cheer,
'Come chase me, pup, I'm over here!'

An ivy whispers sweet little lies,
Saying it's a spy in a donut disguise.
The butterfly laughs, flitting about,
'You're losing your marbles, don't you have doubt?'

A veggie patch dreams of far-away lands,
While I share secrets with leafy hands.
They plotted a journey with no GPS,
Now veggies?'ll drive, in a nightgown no less!

The chairs join in with creaks and groans,
Saying, 'Join our party, leave your phones!'
We'll feast on laughter, in nature's embrace,
With whispers of joy, we'll win this race.

Reclaimed Wilderness of the Heart

A plant was left, just taking space,
It started growing, at its own pace.
We thought it odd, it wore a crown,
Then danced around, as we sat down.

The cat jumped high, in pure delight,
The jungle formed, in the soft light.
With vines that swung and branches stretched,
Our little home, now over-wretched.

Socks have vanished, fate unclear,
Wrapped in green, they disappear.
Our forks now forage through the floof,
In this wild world, we stand aloof.

Yet laughter grows amidst the mess,
In this jungle, we'll confess.
A wild retreat in every room,
With giggles masking nature's bloom.

Fragrant Memories Underneath Our Roof.

Oh, the memories, they smell like spice,
From cookies baked, oh so nice.
Yet dust from plants, they flirt and tease,
With every sneeze, they aim to please.

The potted sage, it tells a tale,
Of relatives who came but failed.
They left their socks, we left our cheer,
Among the stems, the truth is clear.

Chairs are lions, guarding ground,
With foliage behind them, peace is found.
We laugh and cry, it's quite the mix,
In this lush realm, we find our tricks.

Each whiff brings back our dearest past,
Connected here, our roots hold fast.
With every laugh, a memory stays,
Under our roof, in funny ways.

Whispers of Autumn's Embrace

A breeze swept in with tales of cheer,
A leaf went rogue, let's bring a beer!
It danced on the floor, it made a scene,
With friends around, it sparkled green.

The broom chased hard, but lost the fight,
While laughter echoed into the night.
Each crumb confessed, as we all sighed,
Now it's a party, with nature wide!

The window opens, laughter flows,
As twigs invade like wayward prose.
With each bright story, we lose our minds,
In autumn's grip, hilarity binds.

So let's embrace this lively spree,
Where nature shares its company.
As whispers dance and twirls in glee,
We find the fun in greenery!

Vibrant Shadows on the Floor

Sunlight spills, a playful game,
As shadows dance, it's quite the fame.
Who knew a fern could start a show?
With pirouettes, it's all aglow!

Couches sigh, they feel the beat,
With feet that twirl to the leafy heat.
The cat, oblivious, makes its stand,
While hapless hosts just clap their hands.

The rug is waving, riding high,
While snacks are hoarded, oh me, oh my!
With every crunch, a giggle sparks,
As nature hums, in cozy parks.

A puppet show of foliage gleams,
In our wild world, we share our dreams.
With vibrant shadows on the floor,
Life tumbles forth, oh, what a score!

Fragments of Forests Indoors

A fern in the corner does a little dance,
While dust bunnies giggle, given the chance.
With sunlight above, they all take a bow,
Who knew a plant could steal the show now?

The spider plays tag with the leaf on the wall,
While shadows perform an acrobatic sprawl.
A cactus looks smug, standing tall on a shelf,
Daring the others to outshine itself.

In pots they conspire, a secretive crew,
The jokers of nature, the green and the blue.
With each little rustle, a belly laugh grows,
That's just how the wildest of indoor life glows.

So here in this haven of soil and of fun,
The laughter of nature has only begun.
From branches to vines, they're all out to play,
Who knew that the wild could also be gay?

The Quiet Rustle of Change

In the afternoon sun, a sprout starts to sway,
While the cat takes a jump, startling the day.
She lands near the pot of a plant in full view,
Deciding which leaf is the best one to chew.

The coffee cup laughs at the sunlight's bright gleam,
As clutter and chaos create quite the scene.
The rug hums a tune, as plants shake their heads,
"Stop stealing our shine!" they grumble in spreads.

Tangled in vines, we tiptoe with glee,
Avoiding the cactus, it's spiky, you see!
But smiles brighten up when we see what's around,
The mischief of nature is easily found.

With each little rustle, a giggle erupts,
As colorful petals compete to disrupt.
The secrets they share, oh so soft and so sly,
Who knew indoor plants could also tell lies?

Harvesting Presence from Nature

Gather the shadows, let's make some noise,
The succulents whisper, buoyed by the joys.
Each leaf has a secret, a story to weave,
But really it's just that they can't quite believe.

A spider took charge, conducting the breeze,
While houseplants have meetings beneath vines and leaves.
Potted aspirations rise to great heights,
As laughter erupts in the dim of the nights.

Amidst all the chaos, a peace settled down,
As everyone argued who's wearing the crown.
The orchids rolled eyes at the nerdy old sage,
Who spun tales of glory from the garden's great age.

In this fanciful world where the living is bold,
The green crew knows secrets they never have told.
With each rustle and shake, they're having a blast,
The harvest of laughter, forever will last.

Petals and Dreams Intertwined

In a room full of colors, the petals parade,
Each one wearing sunshine, no reason to fade.
The dandelion whispers to roses nearby,
With dreams of the garden, they swear they can fly.

The floor pot is blushing, it caught a good vibe,
As plants swap their stories, their roots start to jive.
A wild flutter here from the cat's endless chase,
As nature laughs on in this cheerful embrace.

Petals look silly with bows on their heads,
Each one of them giggling as sunlight spreads.
They plan a grand party, the plants in full cheer,
A dance on the carpet, oh how they'll endear!

So raise a small toast to the foliage bright,
With petals and dreams taking flight in the night.
For the humor of nature brings joy so divine,
In this lively abode where the green leaves entwine!

Potted Katydids: The House Symphony

In the corner sits a plant,
With a katydid's little chant.
They play their tunes, oh what a feat,
While I try to find my seat.

The dust bunnies join the dance,
In a swirling, wild romance.
Who knew a fern could have such flair,
And turn my couch into a fair?

The vines twist lightly, what a mess,
As the cat joins in, no less.
The curtains sway, the lamp joins, too,
In this symphony of my living room zoo.

And when I sigh that it's too loud,
The plants just giggle, oh so proud.
For who could guess the joyful sound,
Of a house turned into nature's playground?

An Indoor Serenade of Green

A cactus croons, quite out of tune,
While ivy sways to a jazzy tune.
The pothos hangs, a swingy vibe,
As I sip tea, feeling the tribe.

Oh, the table's set for a grand feast,
With snacks for all, even the least!
The orchids join with petals bright,
As we hold our laughter tight.

The palms are clapping, so they say,
As the fish bowl bubbles in ballet.
My socks are gone, the floor's a stage,
In this plant-filled, funny age!

So cheerfully the soil does sing,
A comedy, oh what joy it brings!
Together we weave a quirky show,
In the heart of my home, the pot plants glow.

Flourish Beneath the Eaves

The ferns are gossiping quite clear,
In whispers only I can hear.
They mock the mop, the broom, the dust,
While plotting planty things, they must!

A rubber tree tries stand-up acts,
While succulents exchange their facts.
The coffee cup giggles on the shelf,
As I ponder more of my leafy self.

The spider plant swings with glee,
As I trip over a rogue leaf spree.
Houseplants frown at my bumbling way,
In their indoor cabaret!

So I join the dance, twirl and spin,
And laugh as I coax a frog from within.
Oh, what a party, just look and see,
Beneath the eaves, it's funny as can be!

Rhapsody of Roots and Dreaming Soil

The pot's a stage for root ballet,
As I sip my wine at the end of the day.
With dirt as the backdrop, oh, what a sight,
As the plants all gather for their night flight.

The basil throws leaves like confetti,
While the thyme insists it's far too petty.
A tulip tries a pirouette,
And bumps the shelf, oh what a threat!

In this garden of laughter, I find my grace,
With all my green pals in this shared space.
They whisper jokes beneath lofty lights,
As I'm folding laundry, they take flight.

And as I smile at their nightly spree,
They chuckle quietly, just "wait and see."
For tomorrow the dance will surely renew,
In this rhapsody of roots, with a view!

www.ingramcontent.com/pod-product-compliance
Lightning Source LLC
Chambersburg PA
CBHW072131070526
44585CB00016B/1620